Big Little Voice

COLOURS

the Grey

By M.G. Vaciago

Illustrated by Glen Holman

Matador
9 Priory Business Park,
Wistow Road, Kibworth Beauchamp,
Leicestershire. LE8 0RX
Tel: 0116 279 2299
Email: books@troubador.co.uk
Web: www.troubador.co.uk/matador
Twitter: @matadorbooks

ISBN 978 1800460 669

British Library Cataloguing in Publication Data.
A catalogue record for this book is available from the British Library.

Printed and bound by CPI Group (UK) Ltd, Croydon, CR0 4YY
Typeset in 20pt Blockhead OT by Troubador Publishing Ltd, Leicester, UK

Matador is an imprint of Troubador Publishing Ltd

Dedicated to my son Thomas.

No matter what unkind things
others may say,

follow your own path,

achieve your dreams and

never ever stop shining
as brightly as you do.

I love you x

As I walk home from school,
I spot a bird in a tree.

I wonder what he's thinking,
is he sad, just like me?

Is he sitting there watching a
worm, waiting to swoop?

Or is he friendless and lonely and
been pushed from his birdie group?

I look up to the trees,
standing firm and tall.

How does it work with trees,
do they have friends at all?

Are they nice to each other, as
friendly as can be?

Or does one say to the other,
"Don't you stand next to me"?

The flowers that grow
in the field of grass.

Is one laughed at,
for growing the last?

Is he ashamed that petals
he has none?

Or does he still have a place
standing in the sun?

Is it just kids that are
unkind and cruel?

Are they the exception
and not the rule?

The trees seem imposing,
the birds seem too near,

They all seem to be staring,
I need to get out of here.

"How was your day?"

Mum would quiz.

"It was OK," I'd say, getting in a tizz.

At the thought of going
back again in the morn,

Some days I wish
I'd never been born.

I run up the stairs,
taking them two by two.

I have no idea what I should do.

I slam the door closed behind,

And I'm slowly going out of my mind.

"GO DIE,"

they shout as they laugh in my face.

"You're not special,
a loser and easily replaced.

No-one would miss you
if you would just disappear,

I mean, come on, no-one cares
that you are even here."

So, what if tomorrow
I just didn't wake?

Who would care?
Whose heart would I break?

My mum would cry,
but then she'd be done.

Apart from her,
I don't matter to anyone.

The world would be a better place,

If I wasn't here, taking up space.

I am a no-one, with nothing to give.

I have no future, no reason to live.

That night, as I lie down in my bed,

A glimmer of me appears
over my head.

"Don't be afraid," the voice says,
soft and low.

It was the me I remembered from
years ago.

"My dear friend,"
the voice says. "I see your pain.

And for that reason,
I've come back once again.

To remind you of your worth
and your spirit within,

You must be yourself and not
let the bullies win."

"Don't hide in the shadows,
wishing your days away,

It's your time to be a kid,
have fun and go play.

This bully sees you're funny,
you're brave, you're strong.

He thinks he can break you,
so show him he's wrong."

"It's not true, I'm not brave,"
I say, hiding my face.

"I am a no-one, a loser,
I know my place.

To stay on my own and
do as **I'm** told.

I could never speak up;
I could never be **bold**."

"At lunchtime, I sit on my own
and out of the way,

With every bite I quietly pray,

That he won't find me, and I begin to
eat quick,

And when I see him coming,
I feel really sick."

"He'd laugh and he'd push,
and he'd call me names.

He'd never include me in any of the games.

I'd sit at the back and be
as quiet as can be,

But no matter how I tried,
he'd always notice me."

"As soon as the teacher
turns her back,

The bully is ready and on the attack.

Am I the only one who can see,

How cruel and hurtful
he's being to me?"

"Everyone else in class
doesn't intervene,

And instead they join in with
being mean.

So to the wolves it seems
I have been thrown.

Everyone laughing,
as I stand **alone**."

I shout to the voice,
"Why are you here? Go away.

I'm not interested in what you have to say.

I don't want to dredge up all this pain.

I can't take it; it's making me go insane."

"I will not go," the voice says.
"I'm here for you,

And help you is what I will do.

I am your big little voice,
the positive you from before,

And with your inner strength,
you can be once more."

"What's this?" the voice asks, eyeing a pic,

Of me and my pal when as thieves we were thick,

Before he decided to make me his foe,

and continue to taunt me wherever I go.

"He's no-one," I say, as the photo gets thrown,

To a place and a time before he was known,

Erasing the good and remembering the bad,

Forgetting he was once the best friend I had.

"What is this shining and catching my eye?"
Says my big little voice,
as he saunters by,
To my medals and trophies that
for sports I had won,
In a time when I was happy,
before all this had begun.

"They're the medals I won,
when I used to join in,
But I should now chuck them,
they belong in the bin.
He told me I won them not because
I was fast,
But everyone else was rubbish
and all finished last."

"Have you ever wondered
why he picks on you?

Do you believe what he says
or what is true?

Look around your room and tell me
when you're done.

Just how many awards and medals
you have won."

27

"It's not about you, it never has been.

Your bully has another life,
one you've not seen.

He has worries and issues
he can't surmount,

So, he takes it out on whoever's about."

"Let's take a look at your bully's life,

When he's not causing you
pain and strife.

He's jealous of what you have
and wants it more,

And for that reason,
he kicks you to the floor."

"Close your eyes and let's take a trip.

Take my small hand and
don't lose your grip.

To see the life he tried to conceal,

Let's go and see what's actually real."

"Here we are in 'big man's' place.

Don't worry, don't panic,
he can't see your face.

We are invisible to him, relax,
this time is yours,

To see what really goes on
behind his closed doors."

"Wow, he has all the latest kit,

Laptop, game console and all the bits.

Designer clothes, branded shoes
and more,

Expensive things that I've
never seen before."

"He's trying to do his homework,
but he is stuck,

He knows better than to try his luck,

And ask his parents to explain,

Knowing they'll laugh and call him
stupid again."

"His dad will shout, push and
call him names,

He never hugs or plays some games.

He sits in his room,
crying himself to sleep,

But he can never let anyone
see him weep."

"He comes to school,
feeling alone and weak,

And it's the missing attention
he does seek.

He wants to fill a void and
to feel strong,

So, he picks on you,
even though it's wrong."

"That doesn't excuse what to me,
he has done.

He made my life hell,
when it was supposed to be fun.

He has made me dread every single day,

Worrying about how he'll hurt me
and in what way."

"Those few friends I had,
he managed to drag them along,

When to them I have never done
anything wrong.

He's destroyed me, my strength and my soul.

I'm banished in this anxiety-ridden hole."

"The friends he took are not really his.

Don't be fooled, you see, the reality is,

They're scared of him and stuck to his hem.

If they pretend to be friends,
he won't bully them."

"Don't hate him," the voice says.
"Forgive his evil deeds,

And hope he gets the help he also needs.

Don't hold resentment, anxiety or
hurt in your soul,

Use inner strength and self-worth,
to get you out of this hole."

"I wish I could tell someone
how I feel,

That my feelings of terror are
so very real.

But I'm sure they'd just brush it off
and just say,

'I'm sure it's not that bad,
so just go away.'"

"Close your eyes and think of your class,

When you spoke to your form teacher last.

Imagine you could see her and
she was right here.

Hold my small hand and watch her appear."

"That's Miss Jones, she's my teacher this year.

She's very set on teaching; that's crystal clear.

She is friendly and seems very nice.

She always tells me I can ask for advice."

"So, do you? Ask for advice, I mean?

Or do you just sit there and
try not to be seen?"

"She doesn't mean it,
it's just something you say.

Even if I did, she wouldn't care, anyway."

"Do you remember this happened
after class,

When everyone had left and you
were there last?

She asked how you were and you said, 'All is okay.'

Then you hesitated for a moment, but still walked away."

"You walked away but see you did not,

What happened after.
Do you think she forgot,

About her worries and fears for you?

She was asking everyone's advice
on what she should do."

"He's a bright kid" she says when
she speaks to the head.

"I hear what they're saying,
they're wishing him dead.

He says all is fine,
when I ask him in break,

But I'm scared, he'll have enough
and make a huge mistake."

"I keep it to myself and never complain.

My mum doesn't need any more pain.

She has enough worries and enough stress.

There isn't any way out of this mess."

"My friend, that's not true,
there is always hope.

Remember your worth, and don't sit and mope.

Every problem can be solved, and
solve it you must.

Take a deep breath and tell someone you trust."

"My mum will be mad,
I never said anything before,

But I couldn't land all this at her door.

I see her smile, but I know things are bad,

She's not been herself and she's so very sad."

"She knows you so well, she's known all along,

That something's not right,
but instead very wrong.

She didn't want to push and insist that you tell,

But take the first step to ending this hell."

The stairs look so long and incredibly steep.

I try to slide down them without even a peep,

To where my mum sits, head in her hands.

I'm sure our chat wasn't part of her plans.

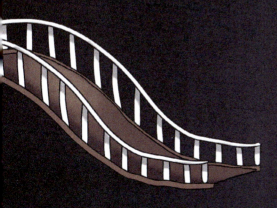

"What's up?" she says, as I walk ever near.

My legs turn to jelly and my face full of fear.

"I need to talk to you," I say, as I
pull up a chair,

My heart pounding and I wonder if I dare.

She takes my hand, as down I sit.

I hold my breath, realising this is it.

The secret I've held on to for so long,

Will soon be out there and soon be gone.

"I'm being bullied," I say, in one fast go.

"I didn't want to tell you, but now you know.

You had so many problems at your door,

I didn't want to land you with any more."

The tears start to stream down her face,

As she takes me in a warm embrace.

Not tears of anger, disappointment,
that scold,

But tears of relief, that I'd finally told.

"My beautiful child,
I've been waiting so long,

For you to tell me what was going on.

So many times, asking I've tried,

But you'd disappear to your room and just hide."

"Yes, it's true, I'm busy and have lots to do,

But that will never be as important as
caring for you.

You're my everything, my pain and my joy.

So, tell me about this bully,
who is this boy?"

Her loving eyes urge me to go on,

And reveal secrets I'd kept for so long.

I open my heart and let it all out,

And finally, she is in no doubt.

"You kept all this from me?" she
says, starting to cry.

"You should have told me, why didn't you, why?"

"I thought you'd either be mad or
think it a joke.

If only I'd known what it would evoke."

"All alone you've carried this pain,

But please, my child, don't do it again.

Come to me, a teacher or a friend.

There is no need to smile and pretend."

"Sadly, bullying goes on all over the place.

It can be as simple as someone not liking your face.

Any difference seems strange to some,

And it's something they just can't overcome."

"Remember the problem isn't yours to fix.

That's the devil on your shoulder playing his tricks.

Making you believe you should no longer be here,

But that's not the case, believe me, my dear."

"That negative voice that's engulfing your head.

Drown it out with positive thoughts and put it to bed.

Remember your worth,
hold your head high,

Work for your dreams and
aim for the sky."

"This bully is threatened by your
tower, and why?

He doubts he could ever build one
that high.

He sees all you've achieved and
all you have done,

So, he decides to break your
bricks, one by one."

"Tomorrow, tell your teachers
what's going on.

I will come with you for support
and urge you on.

They will listen intently,
make sure it's in hand,

Then take a deep breath and
draw a line in the sand."

"Start over with a fire in your chest,

Reach for your goals,
always doing your best.

This bully may come back and
start to jeer,

But remember you're not alone,
for we are all here."

"Now come here, my child, and give me a hug.

Sit next to me, let's get nice and snug.

Remember these words I'm saying to you.

There's a big little voice in your head,
yes, it's true."

"A voice we all have, although some can't hear.

A voice who is brave, when we face fear.

A voice that reminds us who we truly are inside.

A voice that would never tell us to hide."

"Listen to that voice and set yourself free,

And be the best child you can ever be.

This time will pass, and you will grow,

And it will have made you stronger
than you'll ever know."

I give Mum a hug and head off to bed,

Seeing this glowing still above my head.

"I guess that is you that she's talking about.

Your voice is a whisper, so let's teach it to shout."

"Let's do this tomorrow, let's give it our best,

And trust that my mum and teachers do the rest.

Enough of being ashamed of being me,

It's time to shine brightly for all to see."

"A childhood is precious and so live it I will,

I'll be silly and childish, and I won't stop until,

My dreams I've achieved

and my worth I won't hide.

It's me against the world,

with BIG LITTLE VOICE
by my side."

Acknowledgements

This book wouldn't have been possible without the continued support of my husband and my three boys. You guys have been amazing, believing in me from the beginning and never ever doubting me. I love you all so much.

Glen Holman – Thank you for all your support and your incredible illustrations that really brought the characters and the book to life.

A big thank you to Kirsty Harris and Matt Cawley, for reading my first draft and encouraging me to get it published.

Selen Dawson – I can't thank you enough for all your help and support. You helped me work through my own childhood bullying trauma and come out with renewed positivity and enthusiasm.

There are so many more people that I would like to thank for also encouraging me to pursue this dream. They are too many to mention individually, but you know who you are.

About the Author

M.G. Vaciago is a writer of children's books and adult fiction. She is also a wife and a mum of three boys. She is an avid book collector and can't walk past a bookshop without popping in. She created the Big Little Voice series to inspire and empower her children, and in doing so fulfilled a childhood ambition to write books. She is always scribbling down notes about story plots and has a whole world of unwritten books in her head, just waiting to be put to paper.

M.G. Vaciago can be found at

www.mgvaciago.com

About the Illustrator

Glen Holman is an internationally renowned illustrator and book designer whose work has been exhibited in London as well as appearing on Netflix. His life-long passion for illustration started from the moment he held a pencil and has led to the creation of hundreds of books and countless pieces of art. Glen's greatest quality is undoubtedly his intrepid canine companion and noble steed, Winston, the true puppeteer of Glen's success.

Glen can be found at glenholman.com or on Instagram @g.a.holman.